GET CRAFTY

NATURE

Vivienne Bolton

DP

DEMPSEY
PARR

Editor
Barbara Segall

Art Direction
Full Steam Ahead

DesignTeam
Design Study

Photography
Patrick Spillane

Photographic Co-ordinator
Liz Spillane

Styling
Bianca Boulton

Project Management
Kate Miles

The publishers would like to thank Inscribe Ltd., Bordon, Hants. for
providing the art materials used in these projects and
Sophie Boulton for her assistance.

First published in 1998 by
Dempsey Parr
Queen Street House, 4-5 Queen Street, Bath
BA1 1HE

24681097531

Produced by Miles Kelly Publishing Ltd
Unit 11, Bardfield Centre, Great Bardfield, Essex CM7 4SL

British Library Cataloguing-in-Publication Data
A catalogue record for this book is available from the British Library.

ISBN 1-84084-401-9

Printed in Italy

NATURE

Contents

Seedpod Jewelry

Collect seedpods and hollow stalks from the garden in the summer, and stand them up in a jar to dry in a warm airy spot. You will need a large darning needle to make a hole through the seedpods once they have dried. The beads in the necklaces are made from cut lengths of dried stalks. Thread them using the darning needle and decorate them with paint. Gold and brown paint have been used on these beads to accentuate the natural look. Beads painted in bright colors and decorated with glitter would make an attractive necklace.

You will need:

Selection of seedpods and stalks

Scissors

Paint

Paintbrush

Darning needle

Thread

Felt-tip pens

Rubber band

Check with an adult before you pick plants and stems to dry.

1 To make this necklace you will need a few dried hollow plant stems, some small fir-cones and seedpods. Begin by cutting the plant stems into bead-size lengths. Paint the bead lengths, fir cones, and seedpods gold. When your beads are dry, use the darning needle to make suitable holes through them and thread together using one seedpod to every three plant stems to make a necklace or bracelet.

2 This delicate looking necklace is made simply from some dried hollow plant stems. Once you have cut the stems into bead-sized lengths, decorate the beads using brown felt tip pens or brown paint. Thread them together using the darning needle.

3 A small bunch of twigs is used to make this pendant. Choose straight twigs that don't have any thorns or snags. Use a rubber band to hold them together in a neat bunch to form a pendant. Paint the pendant gold; it may be necessary to give it two coats. Once the paint had dried attach a length of thread to the pendant and it is ready to wear.

Birdbath

This mosaic bird-bath would make a good rainy day project. You could use bought miniature tiles or make your own from oven-bake clay like we have. If you make your own tiles you will need to work out the number needed plus a design and color scheme. You could take some inspiration from the color scheme in your garden. Use a tin bowl with a wide lip or ledge for the mosaic pattern. Broken china plates can be recycled to use as mosaic decoration, but ask an adult to assist as the edges can be quite sharp. A mosaic decorated plate would also look good as a houseplant saucer.

You will need:
Oven-bake clay

Rolling pin and knife

Metal plate

Plastic gloves

Spatula

Grout

Cloth

Varnish

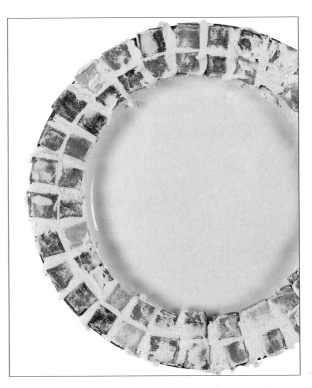

1 Begin by making the tiles using oven–bake clay. Roll out the clay on a clean work surface with the small rolling pin. Cut square tile shapes in your chosen colours to fill the rim of the plate. Harden the tiles in the oven according to the manufacturer's instructions.

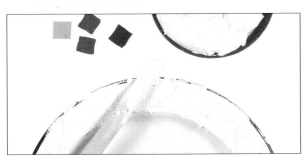

2 When the tiles are ready, make a rough plan of how you will lay them on the plate edge. You will need a metal or china soup plate with a wide raised edge. Put on the plastic gloves and use the spatula to spread a layer of tile grout across the edge of the plate.

3 Press each tile gently into the grout. Leave a narrow space between each tile. You will fill this later. Make sure the tiles all lie neatly along the edge of the plate. Leave to set for 24 hours.

4 When the grout has set use the spatula to fill in with more grout between the tiles. Check that it finishes neatly at the edges and allow it 24 hours to dry.

5 You will now need a cloth to wipe off any excess grout and polish up the tiles. When the tiles look clean, apply a layer of varnish to give them a shine. Let's hope the birds enjoy their new birdbath!

LEAVES, PEBBLES, AND MOSS
Plate Gardens

While away a rainy afternoon making a miniature garden. These realistic-looking gardens are laid out on dinner plates. You could create an imaginary garden or recreate a section of your own garden. Take a look around outside for plants and tiny flowers to use to decorate your plate garden. Make fences from ice-cream sticks or twigs and use your imagination to help you create miniature copies of real-life objects. Use tiny pebbles to make a garden path. See if you can find some miniature ornaments that will be the right scale for garden statues.

You will need:

Plate

Sand

Potting compost

Pebbles

Sticks and thread

Dried flowers and moss

Selection of leaves and flowers

Modeling clay

Salt

Scissors

Paper

1 Place a layer of sand on a plate and cover it with a layer of potting compost. Use small pebbles to lay a path. Make some beanpoles from twigs tied with thread and press them firmly into the earth. Use some moss to create a hedge.

2 The garden is now ready for the vegetables to be "planted." A small-leaved plant stem has been wound round the beanpoles, and a slightly larger leaved plant stem is laid on the earth. The carrot leaves are made from maidenhair fern with clay models of vegetables and garden tools laid among the leaves.

3 The washing is drying in a corner of this sweet little flower garden. Begin with a layer of sand on a plate and cover that with a thin layer of potting compost. Use some checked paper to make the path and two long twigs tied with a piece of string to make the washing line. A piece of paper is cut to make the white picket fence. Now cut some paper clothes to hang on the line.

4 The washing is hung on the line and the garden in now full of flowers and plants. Use moss as plants and some dried flowers pressed into the earth.

5 This winter scene is very effective. Place a layer of sand on the plate and make a snowman from modeling clay. Plant a few moss bushes and press some twigs into the sand. When your model is arranged pour salt over everything to create a snow scene.

Bird Feeders

Whether you live in the town or the country there will be wild birds about. You can easily attract the birds to your garden or windowsill by placing some wild bird seed in a small bird feeder where cats cannot get to it. The birds will enjoy a good meal and you will learn to recognize the different species. The bird feeder is made from an empty milk carton. If you hang it near a window you can keep an eye on the birds while you are out of sight, indoors. You might also want to thread some peanuts on a string and hang them out for the birds.

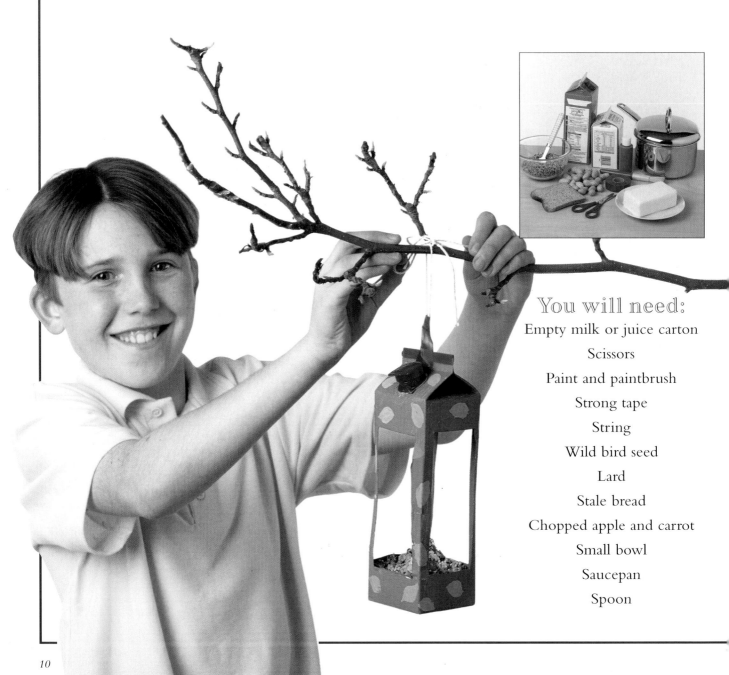

You will need:

Empty milk or juice carton

Scissors

Paint and paintbrush

Strong tape

String

Wild bird seed

Lard

Stale bread

Chopped apple and carrot

Small bowl

Saucepan

Spoon

1 Making this bird feeder is a good way to recycle a milk or juice carton. Cut away most of the sides of the carton leaving space at the base to hold the bird seed.

2 Once you have got the shape of the bird feeder right you can paint it. Choose a color that will blend in with the surroundings and not frighten off the birds.

3 When the paint is dry you can decorate the bird feeder. Attach a piece of strong tape in a loop to the top of the feeder and fill the base with some wild bird seed.

4 Hang your bird feeder in a place, safe from the reach of cats. Thread some peanuts on a piece of string and hang that up alongside the feeder.

5 To make a bird seed ball you will need a saucepan and some lard, available from a supermarket. Melt the lard in a saucepan over a low heat (you may need an adult to help you with this). Collect the rest of your ingredients together. You can use old bread and wild bird seed and could always add some chopped carrot, assorted nuts, or apple to the mixture.

6 Break a slice of bread into small pieces and place them in a bowl; pour over the melted lard. Add the wild bird seed and mix well together. As the mixture cools you will be able to form it into a ball. Push a piece of string into the center of the mixture. Once it has hardened you will be able to hang the ball up with the string, alongside your bird feeder.

Pressed Flowers

Flower pressing was a popular activity among ladies in the nineteenth century. Nowadays flower pressing is regaining popularity as a hobby. If you have a garden it is easy to find flowers to press, although you should check with an adult before you pick any flowers. Pressing flowers dries them out, flattening them and leaving a little of the original color. This creates a material you can use to decorate writing paper and greeting cards, and if you press enough flowers you could create a whole picture or cover a small box. Once you have pressed your flowers, store them flat between layers of tissue paper in a box in a dry, airy place to save their color.

You will need:

Fresh picked flowers to press

Flower press or old book

Scissors

Glue

Items to decorate

When picking flowers to press, make sure that they have no insects in them, and that the petals are perfect, not torn or brown.

Put the flowers in your flowerpress or in tissue between the pages of a thick book, as soon after picking as possible.

1 Pressing flowers is a wonderful hobby. Press the flowers flat in a flowerpress or use an old book. The flowers will need to be left in place for quite a few weeks before they are ready to use.

2 Pressed flowers can be used to decorate greeting cards. You can buy prepared cards to decorate or make your own from nice paper. Spend a little time trying out designs by laying different pressed flowers and leaves on the paper. When you are happy with your design use a little glue to attach the pressed flowers to the card. You may want to paint on a little varnish to give the picture a high gloss finish.

3 For a rose picture, press a whole rose carefully in your flowerpress. Leave it for a few weeks until most of the moisture has dried out. Choose a small frame and place the pressed rose in it. If you press lots of flowers you may have enough to cover a small box.

DRIED FLOWERS AND HERBS
Potpourri

To make your own potpourri you will first need to gather a selection of fragrant petals and dry them in a warm, airy spot away from direct sunlight. Roses and lavender are both very sweet smelling and can easily be grown in a town or country garden. A handful of rose petals can be dried in a paper bag hung up in an airy spot and small bunches of lavender flowers can be hung up on a line to dry naturally in the air. Once you have dried your petals you will be able to mix up some potpourri. You could place bowls of potpourri around a room to make it smell of summer or make some lacy bags to contain small quantities of potpourri to keep your drawers and clothes sweet smelling.

1 To dry rose petals you will need to place them in a warm airy spot away from direct sunlight. If you don't have the space to leave things out put a few petals in a paper bag and hang it up in an airy place. Choose some roses or other flowers which are sweet smelling. Check with an adult before you pick any flowers from the garden.

2 Besides petals you can dry orange and lemon peel, whole small flowers and some leaves. Spices can also be added to dried petals to enhance the perfume of the potpourri. Cinnamon and mixed spice, cloves and nutmeg can all be put in potpourri. If you don't have a flower garden to pick from, you may be able to purchase dried petals from your local wholefood shop. You could ask at the florist for any discarded flowers and buds.

3 One way of making good use of potpourri is to tie it in lace or muslin bags to place in your drawers and cupboards. They will make your clothes smell sweet and some petals and leaves will discourage moths and other unwanted insects from living among your clothes. When, after some weeks the scent fades, fill the bags with newly made potpourri.

Potpourri:

1 cup of fragrant dried rose petals and rosebuds

Half a cup of dried lavender petals

1 cinnamon stick, broken up

A large pinch of cloves

Dried orange peel, broken up

1 teaspoon of sea salt

Mix all the ingredients together in a bowl

You will need:

Dried rose petals and rosebuds

Dried lavender

Selection of dried fragrant leaves and petals

Bowl

Cinnamon sticks

Lace, muslin, and ribbon ·

Needle and thread

Leaf Pictures

I n autumn the leaves on the trees turn from green to brown and all sorts of golden red colors in between. When you are out on an autumn walk collect some leaves of varying shapes, sizes, and colors. At home, press them between the pages of a book. Choose the colors carefully and make sure the leaves you choose don't have tears or holes. When they are dry they still show some of their color. You can then use them as bookmarks on their own and maybe save the best ones to frame as a picture, to hang on a wall, as a reminder of autumn. Try sponging the leaves with gold paint for a good effect.

1 To make a leaf picture choose leaves that have a good shape and color, and are not torn or broken. Carefully place them between the pages of a book and leave for several weeks to flatten and dry.

4 When the black paint is dry, give the leaves an antique metalic look by using a dry sponge with some gold paint. Don't cover the whole leaf with gold paint, make it patchy and interesting.

2 When the leaves are ready, arrange them on a sheet of paper. When you are happy with the picture use glue to hold them in place. Put your picture into a frame.

5 When the gold paint is dry the leaves are ready to be placed in a frame. It may be an idea to collect a selection of leaves from a favorite walk. Press and gild them and when they are framed you can give the picture a title and sign it.

3 In this project the leaf pictures are made more decorative with gold paint, sponged over the leaves. Before you apply the gold, cover the leaves with a layer of black paint.

You will need:

Autumn leaves

Glue

Picture frame

Paintbrush

Black paint

Gold paint

Sponge

Saucer

RECYCLED PAPER
Making Paper

Paper is made from recycled fibrous material—this could be newspaper, computer paper, sugar paper, mashed up potpourri, or leaves. You will need a small picture frame and an adult with a staple gun to help you make a paper making tray. The size of the picture frame will be the size of the sheet of paper you make, so bear that in mind when you choose your frame. Once you have mastered the art of paper-making you can experiment with colors and textures. Try laying pressed flowers on the wet sheet of formed paper or using different colored material. Food coloring can be used to color paper to good effect.

You will need:

Staple gun

Fabric

Wooden picture frame

Torn up pieces of sugar paper

Kitchen blender

Container

Newspaper

Kitchen cloths

Rolling pin

1 To make a paper-making frame ask an adult to staple a piece of fabric taut over the back of a wooden picture frame.

2 Tear the paper up into small pieces and place it in the blender. Cover well with water. Blend until the paper is well mashed. Ask an adult for help with the electric blender.

3 Pour the well watered down paper pulp into a container large enough to take the paper-making frame. You will need enough pulp to half fill the container.

4 Lower the frame into the pulpy water and swish it around getting a layer of paper pulp into the frame. You may need to do this a few times to get the pulp evenly spread across the frame.

5 Lift the frame out of the water. Cover the work surface with old newspaper and lay a kitchen cloth on top of it.

6 In one movement tip the pulp out of the frame. You may need to give the frame a knock to get the pulp out. Place another kitchen cloth on top of the paper and press it down firmly.

7 Press evenly and firmly down on the kitchen cloth using a rolling pin. This will remove the excess water. You have now made a sheet of paper.

8 In this picture there are two sheets of hand-made paper. You will need to practice to get the amounts of pulp right and learn how to spread the pulp evenly across the frame.

OAK-GALLS, FRUITS, AND PETALS
Making Ink

People have been making ink since they could draw and write. Some of the oldest books in existence were written with ink made with oak-galls—try making some for yourself. Oak-galls are the swellings caused by gall wasp larvae burrowing into leaf buds. They are found on oak trees in autumn. Give them a good shake to ensure the insects have hatched and left home. You can also use colored fruit juice as ink—cranberries, raspberries, and cherries all stain in shades of red, while daffodil petals make a yellow ink. If you wanted to be secretive, try writing a letter in lemon juice. Once the writing has dried, you can bring up the message by ironing the paper with a warm iron. The message will color brown and you will be able to read it.

You will need:
Oak-galls, soft fruit, or petals

Pestle and mortar

Jar

Water

Rusty nail

Piece of muslin

Lemon

Paper and pen

1 You will need to find some oak-galls to make this ink. Pick them in the autumn after the insects have flown. Two or three oak-galls will make a couple of tablespoons of ink. Put the oak-galls in a mortar and crush them using a pestle.

2 Place the crushed oak-galls in a jar and add a tablespoon of water for each one and one rusty nail. Leave the mixture to stand, uncovered. After an hour you will notice that the liquid begins to change color. By the next day it should be quite dark and in a week it should be nearly black. Strain the ink through a piece of muslin and it is ready to use.

3 You can use dark colored fruit juice as ink. Use a dipping pen to write with. Cranberries, raspberries, and cherries will give shades of red and you can make a yellow from daffodil petals. Try different vegetables—beet gives a good color.

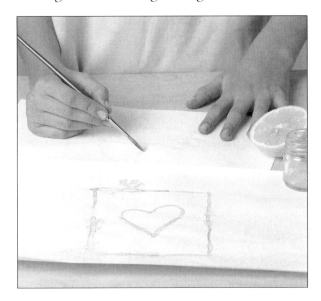

4 To make invisible ink you can use lemon juice. Squeeze the juice of half a lemon into a small container. Use a dipping pen or a thin paintbrush. Write your message on a sheet of paper and leave it to dry. To make the writing visible you will need to iron it, the writing will turn a brown color with the heat from the iron. Ask an adult for help with the iron.

Crunchy Salads

Sprouted seeds make good salads. They are crunchy to eat and packed full of vitamins. You could set up a small sprout farm on the kitchen windowsill and provide the family with fresh salad ingredients all through the winter months. Alfalfa seeds are small and tasty while mung bean seeds are larger. You can sprout sunflower seeds to make large and crunchy sprouts. Ask at your local health food shop for a list of suitable seeds for sprouting.

You will need:

Small piece of muslin

Saucer to draw around

Pen and scissors

Glass jar

Rubber band

Seeds for sprouting

Water

1 To sprout seeds you will need a jar with a muslin lid (so that the seeds can be washed and drained without losing any down the sink). You will need a piece of muslin and a large saucer; use the saucer to mark out a circle on the muslin.

2 Cut away the excess fabric. This will be the lid of the glass jar. You will need a rubber band to hold the fabric onto the jar. You are now ready to start sprouting seeds.

3 Place one large spoonful of suitable seed in the glass jar (we have used mung beans). Cover the seeds with water and leave them to soak for two hours.

4 Lay the muslin over the jar and hold it in place with a rubber band. You will need to rinse away the water. Wash the sprouts with water three times a day and watch them grow. When the sprouts are long enough to eat and before the leaves appear, take them out of the jar. Give them a good wash in clean water and use them in salads for a crunchy fresh taste.

Purchase seeds for sprouting from your local health food shop. Do not sprout seeds purchased for growing in the garden, they sometimes have chemicals on them to prevent pests eating them and can be harmful to people as well.

Twig Furniture

Rustic miniature furniture can be made from twigs and sticks found in the garden. You will need a sturdy pair of scissors and good strong glue for this. A set of miniature garden furniture could be useful when decorating a plate garden, or to sit outside a dollhouse. If you have a miniature teddy bear or doll use it to gauge how large the furniture should be. The early American settlers made real furniture for their cabins from roughly hewn wood. You could make a model cabin and decorate it with rustic furniture and found items from the garden.

You will need:

Sticks and twigs

Kitchen scissors

Glue

Some fabric for cushions or blankets

1 To make the chair you will need some sturdy twigs for the legs and back, and thin twigs to make the seat. It is a good idea to lay the sticks out flat and check their shape. Check that the cut pieces fit together as you go along. When you are happy with the shape of your chair use strong glue to stick it together.

2 For the table choose four good straight twigs to use as legs. Make a frame and glue one leg to each corner. Make the top by laying the pieces down on the work surface and pour a line of strong glue on each end of the tabletop. Leave it to dry. When the frame and the table top have dried you can assemble your table.

3 Make the bed head and foot of the bed first. The bed head is made by making a glued frame with diagonal pieces set in. The foot of the bed is the shape of a letter "H." When the glue has set, fix long twigs between the two ends. Use some fabric to make a mattress and quilt to cover the bed.

Desert Gardens

Growing a desert garden can be most rewarding. Garden centers and florists stock cactus plants. It is a good idea to check what plants are available before you buy a suitable planter. You will need a sunny windowsill on which to place your planted desert garden. Choose a pot large enough to hold a few cacti so that the overall impression is of a small corner of the desert. When you have planted the cacti, decorate the scene with some stones to resemble boulders.

You will need:

Flower pot

Gravel

Old spoon or small garden trowel

Cactus potting compost

Cactus plants

Suitable gloves

Selection of stones and crytals

White sand

1 Begin by placing a layer of gravel. This will provide drainage for the plants.

2 Next add a good layer of suitable cactus potting compost. Press it down firmly.

3 Dig small holes in the compost and plant the cacti. Remember to wear gloves.

4 Create a realistic-looking desert scene with some attractive stones and crystals.

5 When you are happy with the look of your desert garden, cover the compost with a layer of white sand. This will give the impression of desert sand.

Cactus plants need special growing conditions. Keep them hot in summer; place the desert garden on a windowsill that gets sunlight most of the day. Water your plants sparingly and regularly.

Always wear thick gloves when handling cacti as the spines and prickles are sharp.

DRIED LAVENDER, MOSS, AND ROSES
Dried Flowers

Drying flowers is a great hobby. Pick the flowers in summer and hang them up in an warm, dry, and airy place. To prepare them for drying, remove any leaves on the stem and tie them into small bunches or they will dry unevenly. It will take up to three weeks for them to dry. You can use them in a vase or create permanent arrangements of flowers in interesting containers. Dried flowers can also be used to decorate picture frames or make table settings for special occasions.

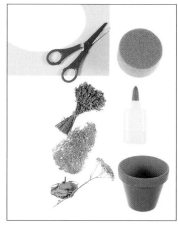

You will need:
Florist's foam

Knife

Terra-cotta pot

A selection of dried flowers

Glue

Scissors

A picture frame

1 Cut the florist's foam to fit. Place it in the flowerpot and press it down well.

2 Place a row of dried lavender bunches around the edge of the pot, pressing them into the foam.

3 Glue an edging of dried moss around the lavender on the edge of the pot. Using scissors, trim off any long or uneven pieces of moss.

4 Use a little glue and place some dried flowers and a dried rose in the center.

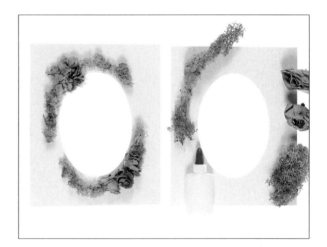

5 To make this a dried flower picture frame you will need a cardboard frame, some dried moss and rosebuds. Begin by gluing the moss around the edge of the oval cut-out. Glue on the rosebuds and leave to dry. A picture frame would make an attractive gift. Offer it with a picture of you in the frame!

Bottle Gardens

Create a miniature oasis in a bottle. All you need to start a bottle garden is a large, empty candy jar and some potting compost. Choose plants which will stay quite small; ask for assistance at your local garden center or florist. Some garden centers have bottle garden departments where they sell small plants suitable for this enclosed, small environment. Bottle gardens should never have the sun shining directly onto them (they would get too hot), but they do need to be in a light situation. Keep the soil moist. You may not need to water often if the lid is kept firmly on. Feed your bottle garden every two weeks during the summer. Decorate it using glass paints and outliners. Choose a gold outliner for a stylish pattern or use black outliner and colored paint to create a stained glass effect on the exterior of the bottle.

You will need:

Sticks

Old spoon

Wire

Kitchen sponge

Cotton wool

A large empty candy jar

Pebbles or gravel

Suitable potting compost

Suitable plants

Glass paints outliner

Glass paint

1 Begin by making some suitable bottle garden tools. For a digging tool, use an old spoon attached with wire to a long stick. Use a piece of kitchen sponge wired onto a stick to press the earth down when you are planting. Lastly, you will need a cleaning tool. For this use a piece of cotton wool wired onto a stick (you may need a few of these to tidy up the bottle garden once it is planted).

2 Place a thin layer of pebbles or gravel in the base of the bottle. This will provide drainage for the bottle garden plants.

3 Cover the pebbles with a thick layer of potting compost. Press the compost down gently using your sponge tool.

4 Use the digging tool to place individual plants in position. Press the compost down firmly around the plants, taking care not to damage their roots.

5 Use the cotton wool tool to clean up the sides of the bottle garden. Wipe away any smears or pieces of compost that have stuck to the sides of the jar.

6 Your bottle garden is now ready to decorate. Choose a simple pattern and mark it out with the outliner. The stained glass effect will resemble a mini-conservatory.

When choosing plants for your bottle garden choose low-growing varieties. Keep the compost moist but do not overwater. Feed your bottle garden every two weeks in the growing season.

Index